I0786260

Justice for Bobbi Kristina

O.D.H Taylor

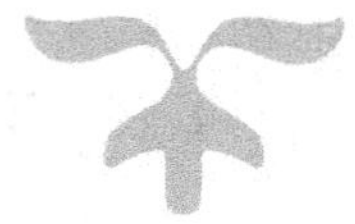

APRIL 8, 2018
HSC SUGARLAND PUBLICATIONS

Chapter One

Unconscious and Unresponsive

In the world of psychology and from the words of the famous Dr. Phil, it is said that, "the best predictor of future behavior is past behavior". In layman's terms, "a leopard never changes its spots", only means a person is bound to repeat behavior in which he or she once engaged. The point of this discourse is the interpersonal behavior of Nick Gordon, in his relationship with women, is apparently questionable. In the relationship with both Bobbi Kris and Laura Leal, his true colors shine brighter than the majestic colors of the

Bobbi Kris, Forever

rainbow. Nick Gordon appears to be very controlling and domineering of the women he dates.

Indicators of Intimate Partner Violence are manifesting and reflecting that Nick Gordon is abusive to the women he allows to be a part of his life. The alleged domestic violence accounts of what happened to Bobbi Kristina, just a few short years ago, in 2015, is beginning to repeat itself in the relationship with Laura Leal. The young Laura Leal is too subjectively involved in the relationship with Nick Gordon to heed the advice of family, friends and the Courts. Everyone is telling Laura Leal that she is in a dangerous situation; but she can't or refuse to hear them. The domestic violence warning signs are glaring her right in the face; but, she is ignoring the flashing lights of danger that confronts her. Many women have died because of intimate partner abuse (domestic violence) in the United States. I am praying that Laura Leal does not become another statistic due to naivety; yet, there are various indications that she is on a path of self-destruction or destruction at the hands of a man.

This is not a story of Whitney Houston's addiction to drugs, nor is the focus on the substance abuse that adversely affected the lives of Bobbi Kristina, her mother or her father. Focusing on the substance abuse only muddies the water and deflect from the real issue of the domestic violence that contributed to the death of a very young Bobbi Kris.

Bobbi Kris, Forever

After all, if the family was not famous, the substance abuse part of the story would have been long forgotten by now. Many American families are suffering from the consequences of substance abuse. Likewise, many Americans have friends who are substance abusers. Furthermore, many Americans are substance abusers themselves or have abuse substances in their past lives. Retrospectively, the substance abuse that devours families is not a new phenomenon; thus, substance abuse should not be the focus of what happened to Bobbi Kris. Instead this is a tragic account of a young woman, in the prime of her life, who has received very little justice for her questionable demise.

Bobbi Kris, Forever

Born with the proverbial silver spoon in her mouth, Bobbi Kristina Brown was the daughter of singers, Whitney Elizabeth Houston and Bobby Brown. In 2012, due to the untimely and unfortunate death of her famous mother, Bobbi Kristina was faced with the overwhelming hardship of growing up fast. Shielded by her mother, most of her life, she had very little experience or exposure to what the real world could be like; especially, if you are both rich and famous. She had no idea of the parasitic behaviors of people who can show alliance on the one hand, yet could turn on you as soon as they are not getting their way. The bible names this type of person as a "sheep in wool clothing." This type of person is the very one who

Bobbi Kris, Forever

claims to love you; yet, would physically harm you at the loss of a dime. She had no idea that she would find these characteristics in someone she called, "my husband." It is sad that her first encounter with love, would end in such a tragic manner.

Unfortunately, almost three years to the date of her mother's death, Bobbi Kris faced an almost identical tragedy. She was found unconscious, on January 31, 2015, in a bathtub of water, faced down, and barely clinging to life. The only difference between the two deaths was Whitney died on the same day of her drowning; while, Bobbi Kristina lingered for many months, in a medically induced coma; as, the medical staff tried to save her life. She officially succumbed to lobar pneumonia,

Bobbi Kris, Forever

caused by hypoxic encephalopathy (lack of oxygen to the brain) resulting from water immersion and drug intoxication.

When the story was first released that the daughter of Whitney Houston had been found unconscious in the bathtub, the first thought was Bobbi Kris was trying to commit suicide. "How ironic was it that she was found in the bathtub, drowned like her mother?" It was way too eerie that mother and daughter were both found immersed in water in a bathtub. With their lives so closely intertwined and the emotional destitution faced by Bobbi Kristina because of Whitney's death, it would lead one to think that she no longer wanted to live on earth without her mom.

Bobbi Kris, Forever

Look at the facts, around the same time she was found in the bathtub, was around the same time the Lifetime movie, about her mother, was making its debut. Any young adult, not yet over the death of her mother, would be devastated by the debut of a movie that showed both the positive and negative aspects of her mother's life. However, listening to the many accounts of her last days before she was found unconscious, indicated that she had every reason to want to live. As the account goes, Bobbi Kristina was planning to go to California to start her music career. It doesn't appear that this was a young woman who wanted to end her life. Grief stricken, yes, but she was not assumed to be a suicidal woman at all. Still Leola Brown, the sister of Bobby

Bobbi Kris, Forever

Brown, predicted that Bobbi Kristina should be very cautious because someone would be coming to kill her next.

So, how did Bobbi Kris become unconscious in a bathtub, filled with water? Did Nick Gordon, hurt and then attempt to drown her? According to her friends, on the evening before she was found unconscious, Nick had come home from the nightclub heavily intoxicated. Although the details are sketchy, on the Dr. Phil Show, it was said, by Nick's mother, that Max Lomax, Nick Gordon and Bobbi Kris came home from a party or nightclub in the wee hours of Saturday morning. Nick went into the room to go to bed and Bobbi Kristina went to take a bath. Yet, other media accounts proclaimed,

Bobbi Kris, Forever

Bobbi Kris and Nick had a terrible argument that led to him dragging her up the steps. They continued to argue and suddenly, the argument quelled. Nick, then went to get into bed with Danyela Bradley and said something to the effect of wanting a cute little white girl now. How disrespectful was this to Bobbi Kristina and the memory of Whitney-the one person who took him into her home when he and his mother were estranged? Retrospectively, these events alone really attest to Nick Gordon's character.

Further, media reports revealed in the later hours of the morning, during a visit from a cable representative, Krissi was mysteriously found unconscious and faced down in the bathtub by Max

Bobbi Kris, Forever

Lomax. He lifted her out of the bathtub, and then called for Nick Gordon; who performed CPR until the paramedics arrived to transport Bobbi Kris to the hospital. Similarly, it was also mentioned on the Dr. Phil Show, that on the day of Whitney's death, Nick proclaimed to have performed CPR on her; yet, the Houston family maintains he never performed CPR on Whitney. What are we to believe now? Is it practical to tell an alleged untruth when suspicion already looms thickly over Nick's head like a dark cloud on a rainy day? What was the purpose of the alleged lie? But most importantly, what happened between the time of the quarrel, the quelling of the spat and then, Bobbi Kris' immersion in a tub filled with water?

Bobbi Kris, Forever

Also, based on media reports, there was a dustpan found in the bathtub. So, why was a dustpan found in the bathtub with Bobbi Kris? Who takes a bath with a dustpan? This isolated piece of information, lends suspicion to the entire trajectory of events that occurred on January 31, 2015. Still to this date, there has been no justice for Bobbi Kristina Brown. There have been no charges brought against Nick Gordon for his alleged physical attacks on Bobbi Kristina, either.

Every attempt has been made by Bobby Brown, her father, to bring Nick Gordon to justice or to at least have questions answered by her ex-boyfriend. The opportunity for Nick to explain and defend what happened on January 31st would have been at

Bobbi Kris, Forever

the civil court hearing. He could have cleared up all doubts at that hearing. However, he continued to avoid appearances in court which made him look even more suspicious. Would you have tried to clear your name at the first opportunity possible? It is befuddling why Nick continues to hide instead of exposing the truth to her family; especially her father.

Imagine the telephone ringing and someone on the other end of the phone is telling you that your daughter has drowned in the bathtub? One of the first things, any parent would want to know is simply, "What happened?" It doesn't matter that its Whitney Houston's daughter or Bobby Brown's daughter or the way they lived their lives. All that

Bobbi Kris, Forever

really matters is that its someone's child, who was in dire straits. Someone's grown child, has been found in a bathtub filled with water, faced down. Logically, the first question should be "How does a grown woman become immersed in water face down?" When we, as humans, get into a tub of water, we sit first. Then, we lay back with the front of our body faced up; not, down! We are not swimming, we are taking a bath or relaxing in the tub faced up! So then, the question becomes, after finding her is such an awkward position, "Did she fall forward due to intoxication?" This is logically possible, but if so, "Why didn't Nick Gordon just answer Bobby Brown's questions about his daughter?" The question again being "What

Bobbi Kris, Forever

happened to my daughter?" The events surrounding

this aspect of what happened to Bobbi Kris are so

bizarre-undoubtfully, suspiciously devious!

Chapter Two

The Vigil

The "Shining a Light for Healing" vigil was held in Bobbi Kristina's honor on February 9, 2015. The public was invited to come to the Riverdale Town Center Amphitheatre in Georgia to pray for Bobbi Kris who was on life support. The amphitheater is in front of City Hall at the Riverdale Town Center.

Bobby Brown did not attend the ceremony, but his siblings were present at the event. Whitney Houston's family were not in attendance at the vigil, either. Approximately three hundred fans and friends joined the vigil to pray for Bobbi Kristina Brown. She had been on life support for nine days, at Emory University Hospital, and it was hoped that the prayers would help to save her life. Although the family reported that she was fighting for her life, they remained hopeful that she would recover. Tommy Brown, brother of Bobby Brown, asked Bobby and Whitney Houston fans and friends to "Just keep your prayers up for Bobbi Kris."

It was an evening of speeches, songs, dance and prayers. The Mayor of Riverdale, Evelyn Wynn-Dixon, joined the vigil by singing a gospel song and speaking to the crowd of participants. She let the invitees know that although the family had been blessed in a lot of ways, they face as many hardships as anyone else. She let the crowd know that this families' pain is no different than the pain

Bobbi Kris, Forever

that is experienced by all human beings. The Mayor said, "They bleed and hurt like us."

Another notable citizen, Corey Punzi organized the vigil at the amphitheater because Bobby Brown was the first artist to perform there when it first opened. Therefore, the Riverdale Community wanted to show support for Bobbi Kristina and the family in their trying times. The Mayor and City Council promised to be available to Bobbi Kristina's family for whatever they needed. Further, poignant words of comfort were spoken by Pastor Dukes who said, "Whether she wakes up or not, God has her and she's going to be good either way."

Bobbi Kris, Forever

At the time of the vigil no one knew what the outcome of the coma would be. Everyone was just praying for a miracle. A miracle that would never come in the form of a young woman living her life into old age. The only miracle that did emerge was God saw Bobbie Kristina suffering through a coma and pneumonia, and came for his child.

She would forever be young; always a 22-year-old, in the minds of those who knew and loved her. Always, a 22-year-old to those who never had the opportunity to meet her. Always the 22-year-old who never experienced the full potential of her dreams.

Bobbi Kris, Forever

Yet, she leaves a legacy that is a cautionary tale for the young women of her generation. The tale is not of money and the spoils of riches. Money and things are material, and as the bible states, "will fly away."

The tale is one of the wisdom every young woman should behold regarding her life. This cautionary tale tells everyone that Bobbi Kris tried to separate herself from Nick Gordon when she was unhappy in the relationship. She had every right to make that decision, like any other young woman.

Every young woman should first understand that if a relationship is unhealthy and causing unhappiness, leave immediately! Do not stay in a

Bobbi Kris, Forever

situation that is going to lead to additional problems in life. No one has the right to punch, curse or abuse anyone. The second lesson should always be, when things begin to go wrong, in the relationship, let family know and keep family around always. Do not keep secrets from family because of embarrassment. Family will take care of, and protect you. Third, go to the police and let it be known, you are a victim of domestic violence and if you can move, move fast! Do not continue to live with someone that doesn't have your best interest at heart. Always remember that you are an individual first and someone's partner afterwards. Finally, keep your financial business guarded. People become someone different when there is money

Bobbi Kris, Forever

involved and if you are blessed enough to have a lot of it, guard yourself cautiously. Learn these lessons well and Bobbi Kristina's life will continue to shine and help other young women through similar circumstances.

Bobbi Kris, Forever

Chapter Three

Analysis of Nick Gordon on the Dr. Phil Show

Nick Gordon threatened to kill himself when talking to his brother over the phone. He said he had taken Xanax and Unisom. He regurgitated the pills before he could commit suicide. Did he really want to kill himself or was it an act to cover up a guilty conscious for what he had done to Bobbi Kristina? Was his supposed suicide attempt a means of gaining sympathy from his mother and the world of viewers of the Dr. Phil show?

Whatever the reason, he was so convincing that his biological mother, Michelle Gordon, contacted Dr. Phil McGraw for help.

Bobbi Kris, Forever

On the day of the show, Michelle Gordon arrived without Nick knowing that she was going to be there, too. She revealed, Nick felt guilt and pain about Krissi current illness and Whitney's death in 2012. Nick divulged, to his mother, that he promised Whitney that he would protect Krissi. The impact of the of events leading to Bobbi Kristina's medically induced coma was taking its toll on Nick, she explained, to Dr. Phil and the viewers. He was convinced that if he could only talk to her she would wake up and recover. He blamed Bobby Brown for not letting him see Bobbi Kristina; yet, he was unwilling to talk to her father about the incident. Further, he arrived at the Dr. Phil Show, presenting himself, as too intoxicated to talk.

Bobbi Kris, Forever

So, let's make the first analysis of what Michelle

Gordon has disclosed thus far. Based on the

statement that Nick felt guilty because he promised

Whitney that he would take care of Krissi, is a

heavy burden for any individual to carry on his

shoulders. At 21 years old, Krissi had the

responsibility of caring for herself. She had an

allowance from her inheritance, so financially she

did not have to face the hardships that most 21-

year-old, young adults, face when they are out on

their own for the first time. She could have used the

emotional support because she had lost her mother

tragically; but, how much emotional support was

being provided to Bobbi Kris. Emotional support

consists of love, warmth, caring and good

Bobbi Kris, Forever

advisement. Was Krissi receiving this type of support from Nick? Not at all; instead, she as receiving emotional and physical abuse while he was spending her money.

The second analysis focuses on what Michelle Gordon revealed when she said that Bobbi Kristina's medically induced coma was taking its toll on Nick because he couldn't see Krissi. Any descent human being would be upset by the hospitalization of their significant other. This is human nature to be caring about the conditions that affects someone we love. But what's really behind the exaggerated behaviors of Nick Gordon regarding this unfortunate incident. By the time Nick Gordon made his first appearance on the Dr.

Bobbi Kris, Forever

Phil Show, Bobbie Kristina had been in a coma for several months. The mind adjusts to difficult situations within a certain period and our coping mechanisms kick in to help us deal with the situations that confront us. Although alcohol and Xanax were a factor in his emotional display, his level of maturity also played a role in the emotional upheaval that was witnessed on public television. Perhaps, this need to be the center of attention, as evidence by telling Dr. Phil he was making him famous, and the very dramatic, on stage, outpouring of emotional display, is a personality disorder. Specifically, the behavior is indicative of histrionic personality disorder.

Bobbi Kris, Forever

Another point of analysis focuses on Nick Gordon's hatred of Bobby Brown. On the show, one of the most poignant declarations that Nick made, occurred when he cried out "I hate Bobby Brown." Based on the historic account of Bobbi Kristina's estranged relationship with her father, for a period, after Whitney died, when did Nick Gordon have the opportunity to be around Bobby Brown to develop any type of emotions for or against him? Even before Whitney died, Nick Gordon had no contact with Bobby Brown to have any kind of emotions for him, good, bad or indifferent. If Nick developed negative emotions about Bobby, these emotions were based on what he heard from Whitney and Bobbi Kristina. So, this was another measure of

Bobbi Kris, Forever

deflection, a defense mechanism to decrease anxiety related to the guilt he was experiencing about the questions that were bound to be asked by Dr. Phil. Moreover, he did not hesitate to place blame onto Bobby Brown, when he was not even present when the incident occurred with Bobbi Kristina. In fact, her father was in another state when she was found in the bathtub.

Gordon was manipulating Bobby Brown's bad boy image based on how he believed the public felt about Bobby and the fact, that Bobby was arrested numerous times for behaviors that were related to addiction. Nick knew that the public loved Whitney for her talent and public image…the good girl, church going, image. So, he tried to play on the sympathy of the public, not considering that he, like

Bobby, have a bad boy image, too.

Yes, substance abuse directly and indirectly affects the lives of the substance abuser and their children; but there comes a time when every individual must accept responsibility for what they do in life. This is where the healing begins, through acceptance and change. Instead of placing blame, this was Nick's opportunity to square things with Bobby. Even if he didn't want to be in the room alone with Bobby Brown, he could have requested that Dr. Phil serve as the mediator between the two of them. Further, based on the premise that he was so upset because Bobbi Kris was in a coma, why not release the anxiety he was feeling by giving

Bobbi Kris, Forever

Dr. Phil and the viewers the answers that was sought?

The fourth point of analysis centers on Nick's belief that if he could only see and talk to Bobbi Kris, she would wake up and recover. The idea, was indicative of someone with a narcissistic personality disorder. In this disorder, a person view himself as someone who is very important and with a sense of entitlement. People with this disorder are grandiose, manipulative, self centered and demanding. If the family members, who had known Bobbi Kristina all her life, could not awaken her from a medically induced coma, how could Nick?

Bobbi Kris, Forever

Mr. Gordon set the tone and atmosphere for the Dr. Phil Show. Dr. Phil had an agenda to discuss the details of what happened on January 31, 2015. Nick Gordon had another agenda. He had no intentions of having the conversation about what happened to Bobbie Kristina at all; hence, the reason for the drunken stupor to detract from the real reason for his appearance on the show. And what a show he gave to the entire world.

Although Nick appeared to be intoxicated, his behavior was so erratic that one would question his level of intoxication. Some of his actions appeared to be contrived and not indicative of someone who had taken Xanax. Xanax is a benzodiazepine that slows down the central nervous system; like, the

Bobbi Kris, Forever

alcohol he also ingested. Both drugs, alcohol and Xanax have a calming and sedating effect on the body. So why was Nick bouncing around the stage, unable to stay seated or to answer the questions posed to him by Dr. Phil? Was he afraid that the words that he would say on public television would come back to haunt him in court? Better yet, was he afraid that the public would assume he was taking cocaine, too?

Nick came on stage, crying and saying that he would never hurt anyone. He maintained that he did not hurt Krissi; but his mother, nor did Dr. Phil have the opportunity to ask him if he had hurt anyone. In psychology, we call this type of unbridled response, projection. He was reacting as if he anticipated the

Bobbi Kris, Forever

questions that were not asked of him yet. These feelings were Nick's unconscious feelings that he was projecting to relieve his anxiety. An anxiety rooted in the painful thought that something had happened to Bobbi Kristina that he had a hand in, but refused to acknowledge. Perhaps this lack of acknowledgement is associated with denial, fear or the fact that he broke a promise to take care of Krissi; and, instead caused her insurmountable emotional and physical pain.

Dr. Phil, changed his platform, when no other opportunity was available to interview Nick, to stage an intervention for him. The purpose of the intervention was to get Nick to enter treatment to become sober enough to save his life, but, also so that he could answer questions about Bobbi Kris. When Dr. Phil went to the room to get Nick and to bring him on stage. Nick rush down the hall as if he was feeling the effects of cocaine instead of Xanax. Dr. Phil had to prompt him to slow down. At this point, the real drama begins.

Nick bounced on the stage, see his mother, run to hug her and speaks in an infantile voice, "Mommy, oh my gosh, oh my gosh, oh my gosh, Mommy, I am so sorry for everything. Alright, alright let's do this. Mom I would never hurt anybody. I like, I love people. Alright, so here we go!" Throughout this portion of the show he portrays himself in an infantile state; one without any control over his life and circumstances.

Okay! So, what does Nick have to be sorry about?

If, in fact, an accident had occurred, because Krissi was intoxicated, and had slipped under the water while in the tub, would this be Nick's fault? Not at all!   It would have been viewed as an unfortunate accident that had happened because friends had partied a little too much and one of them decided to take a bath, fell asleep and slipped under the water while in the tub. Simply, an unfortunate accident would have been the consensus. But is this the way that it actually happened? Probably not!!

Bobbi Kris, Forever

And is this the true reason that Nick was so upset

because he knows more happened than he is willing

to admit. It appears that there is so much more to

the story than is being told. So much more!!

Bobbi Kris, Forever

Chapter Four

Multiple Beatings and the Civil Lawsuit

It seems that Nick Gordon had a hatred and jealousy for Bobbie Kristina; instead, of the adoration a young man should have for the woman he admires and loves. Although their intimate relationship was less than three years old, assaults against her were numerous. He proclaimed an overwhelmingly passionate love for Bobbi Kris, but his behavior indicated otherwise. Days before the January 31, 2015 incident, that left Bobbi Kristina unconscious and unresponsive, Nick Gordon attacked her.

Friends were hanging out with Bobbi Kristina in her Georgia townhome. They witnessed, Nick Gordon jump on Bobbi Kris and hit her in the face so hard, the living room sofa had broken. Subsequently, he knocked her on the floor, beat her in the face and then kicked her in the side. During this altercation he knocked the first tooth out of her mouth. Screaming and in excruciating pain, she was unable to get off the floor to go upstairs when he commanded her to do so. So, according to the court files, he dragged Bobbie Kris up the stairs by her hair. She was so bloody that splatter was found on the walls of her townhouse.

In another incident, on the morning of January 31, 2015, Nick was out clubbing, drinking and on a

Bobbi Kris, Forever

cocaine binge, hours before an altercation began between him and Bobbi Kristina. When he arrived home, around 6 am, he checked the security camera footage and apparently did not like what he saw and heard on the footage. Nick accused Bobbi Kristina of cheating on him. He and Bobbi Kristina began to argue from the kitchen, into living room, and then into the bedroom. He inflicted emotional abuse on Bobbi Kris by calling her derogatory names, like "bitch" and then, "whore". The argument was loud and then, it abruptly ended. Bobbi Kristina was later found unresponsive and unconscious, face down in the bathtub, with her mouth swollen and another tooth knocked out. She was transported to the hospital and placed in a medically induced coma

Bobbi Kris, Forever

and never recovered. Bobbi Kristina died six

months later in hospice.

Before Bobbi Kristina died, a civil lawsuit was

filed against Nick Gordon by Bedelia Hargrove,

Court Appointed Conservator. She filed a civil

lawsuit, against Nick Gordon on June 24, 2015 in

Fulton County, Georgia.   The details of the original

court file enumerated the various counts of claims

against Nick Gordon because of what he had done

to Bobbi Kristina. The papers opened with the

different types of relationships, Nick had with her

through the years. It declared that there was a time,

when Nick considered himself Bobbi Kris' brother

(before the death of Whitney Houston), then he

became her boyfriend (after the death of Whitney)

and finally, he was considered her husband as of

January 9, 2014. At the point of being considered

her husband, it specified, that Nick Gordon had

begun to control her.

The court document encompassed seven counts

of misconduct against Nick Gordon to include:

Count One: Assault, Count Two: Battery, Count

Three: Intentional infliction of emotional distress,

Count Four: Conversion, Count Five: Unjust

enrichment, Count Six: Attorney Fee's and Count

Seven: Punitive damages.

On the Count One Assault claim, it was detailed

that Nick Gordon attacked and abused Bobbi

Kristina Brown with the intent to cause her

apprehension of a violent injury. It further denoted that the wrongful misconduct of Nick Gordon was intentional, reckless and grossly negligent. Because of the unknowing, willful, intentional, reckless and grossly negligent behavior, Bedelia Hargrove was requesting at least 10 million dollars as a reward for punitive damages.

Next, on the Count Two Battery claim, it was alleged that Nick Gordon intentionally engaged in and caused unwanted, harmful and offensive bodily contact to Bobbi Kristina Brown. The document proclaimed that Bobbi Kristina suffered substantial bodily harm to include the loss of teeth, pain, suffering and trauma because of Nick Gordon's physical abuse of her. As a consequence of this

Bobbi Kris, Forever

knowing, willful, intentional, reckless and grossly negligent behavior, Bedelia Hargrove was requesting at least 10 million dollars as a reward for punitive damages.

Third, on the Count Three, Intentional Infliction of Emotional Distress, the document denoted that Bobbi Kristina suffered extreme visible life altering bodily harm because of Nick Gordon's outrageous, unwanted, harmful and offensive contact. It maintained that because of this behavior, she suffered severe emotional distress. Again, because of the unknowing, willful, intentional, reckless and grossly negligent behavior, Bedelia Hargrove was requesting at least 10 million dollars as a reward for punitive damages.

Bobbi Kris, Forever

On Count Four, Conversion, the assertion was Nick Gordon, without authorization, transferred money from Bobbi Kristina's bank account to his bank account while she was in a medically induced coma. Although she could not demand her property back, it was known by family and friends that he took money from her. According to the document, he never returned the money to her account. As a result of the Conversion, the document further explained, that Bobbi Kristina suffered damages and should be awarded punitive damages in the amount of at least ten million dollars.

Next, Count Five, Unjust Enrichment, the court document maintained Nick Gordon was enriched by money transferred from Bobbi Kristina's account. It said that he had benefitted and will continue to benefit from the personal property and trust assets of Bobbi Kristina. This unjust enrichment had damaged Bobbi Kris.

Count Six, Attorney Fees, espoused that Nick Gordon had been stubbornly litigious, had acted in bad faith and had put Bobbi Kristina and her attorney through unnecessary trouble and expense.

The Seventh Count, Punitive Damages, highlights the intentional disregard of the rights of Bobbi Kristina Brown and the well-deserved damages, in an amount determined by the court. Again, within this count, Bedelia Hargrove noted

Bobbi Kris, Forever

that Nick Gordon's conduct was intended to cause physical harm. The amount of punitive damages was to be determined by a jury of her peers.

Nick Gordon was going to answer to somebody about the incident, in one way or another. Bedelia Hargrove was not falling victim to his games or shenanigans. She had systematically planned the most supreme retribution against Nick Gordon; one that threatened to unravel every thread of his total being. He had finally met his match and she never laid a finger on him. Bedelia, next friend, showed herself as a worthy contender. She used the power of her mind to entrap Nick Gordon in a manner he never saw coming. She aimed to hit him in the

pocket and make it difficult to survive in this
country.

Chapter Five

Memorializing Krissi

Saturday, August 1, 2015 was a sad and extremely hard day for the Houston and Brown families. Bobbi Kristina had gone to glory, and it was now time to honor her very short life. When someone dies naturally, there is an unbelievable sadness that encircles the soul of those left behind. Contrarily, when someone passes on because of tragic circumstances there is a perpetual gloom that shadows family members everywhere they go. Emotions run high and unforgivable words are exchanged.

Bobbi Kristina's silver casket arrived to the St. James Methodist Church in Alpharetta, Georgia. The Brown and Houston families entered the church to say goodbye and celebrate the life of their "little princess." Arriving in a motorcade of limousines, notable celebrities were among the invited guests and friends to attend the service. Secured checkpoints, on the route to the church, ensured that no unwanted people would intercede in the service.

The memorial service processional opened with the singing of the "Holy Lamb of God" by the St. James Mass Choir. From the Old Testament, there was the reading of Psalm 23 by Reverend Billy House; while Bishop TD Jakes preached from the New Testament. Monica sang the Whitney Houston

Bobbi Kris, Forever

classic, "I Love the Lord". Expressions of love and honor was delivered by Dr. Shirley Shields. The service continued with Bobbi Kristina's godmother, CeCe Winans singing "His Strength is Perfect." Family and friends offered words of expressions in memory of Bobbi Kris. Kim Burrell sang "Take me to the King". Tyler Perry and Rayah Houston memorialize Bobbie Kris in heartfelt expression.

The celebration was running smoothly until Pat Houston walked to the dais to venerate Bobbie Kristina with expressions of love from the family. At the point she had begun to speak, Bobbie Brown's sister, Leolah Brown, began to yell out during the service. With emotions running high on this bleak day, it was no wonder that heated words

Bobbi Kris, Forever

were spoken. It was reported by various media outlets that the disturbance led to security descending upon Leolah Brown as she left the house of worship.

Outside the church, Leolah gave the media an account of what had happened to cause her to leave the memorial service. According to Leolah Brown, everything was going fine with the service until Pat Houston started to speak and she didn't like it. She told Pat, that Whitney would haunt her from the grave. She further went on to say that she is going to expose Pat Houston for "who she really is". She further elucidated she would be doing interviews in the days ahead. Leolah maintained the feud between the Houston's and the Brown's was not over and wouldn't be over for a long time.

The remaining part of the service ended smoothly. The traditional repast, as celebrated by African Americans, followed the service. The theme was reported to be in the tradition of the sweet sixteen party she never had. People who knew her and people who never met Bobbi Kris carried heavy hearts on this day.

Nick Gordon tried desperately to attend the funeral service for Bobbi Kristina. In his plead to attend the service, he wrote "I love Krissi with all my heart and I am destroyed that she is gone, and I need to say goodbye." He further stated, "I'm

Bobbi Kris, Forever

begging both of you (speaking to Pat Houston and Bobby Brown via email) to please put your differences aside and allow me this chance. Krissi loved me very much and she would want me there. Please consider this?"

Though these expressions were his requests, he was not allowed to attend the memorial service for Bobbi Kristina Brown. People magazine reported that he was begging and pleading to attend the service. Reportedly, the email he sent to both Pat Houston and Bobby Brown, went unanswered. Thus, Michelle Gordon, told People magazine that Nick honored Bobbi Kristina's memory at the beach. He decided, since he couldn't attend the service at the church, then he would go to the place they both loved…the beach.

Love comes in many forms. Passionate love has both a positive and negative side to it. It is the type of love that makes young people believe they can't live without each other. It is the kind of love expressed in the need to spend every waking moment with each other. It is what psychologists and therapists deem an immature love. When expressed positively, it can feel so good; conversely, when expressed negatively, it can hurt so badly.

A person who physically abuse a loved one may think this is the appropriate way to express love for

Bobbi Kris, Forever

someone. Moreover, to withhold information from people you want to consider your family, does not require that guns are brandished. Nor does it require that the person considered to be a significant other or "wife" be isolated from family. It most certainly does not mean that drugs are brought or shared in the relationship; instead, it means the loved one is convinced to enter a rehabilitation facility to receive assistance. Finally, it doesn't mean that the person's money is transferred from her account without permission.

The true meaning of love is written in the bible:

"Love is patient, love is kind and is not jealous; love does not brag and is not arrogant; does not act unbecomingly; it does not seek its own, is not provoked, does not take into account a wrong suffered, does not rejoice in unrighteousness, but rejoices in the truth; bears all things, believes all things, endures all things. Love never fails".

Did Nick Gordon love Bobbi Kristina Brown? The only response a well-trained therapist can give is, not in a healthy way. Love allows a person to be free in the space that she needs, when she needs it. Instead of the fear that permeated his heart and mind, Nick Gordon should have given Bobbi Kristina the space she needed to grow within the dimensions of her uniqueness. Although we all have a need to be admired and loved, this doesn't mean take possession of the very essence of who a

Bobbi Kris, Forever

person is individually. A partner who is the best person she can be for herself first, will make a better and more secure partner in the future. Everyone is entitled to their individuality and space. No one, who is secure within himself, should feel threaten because his mate wants to leave. It was once said, "If you love someone, set her free and if she comes back, she is yours."

Heed these words and if it is impossible to do so, it is time to see a therapist.

Chapter Six

The Autopsy Report

Many questions abounded as the family, friends and public waited impatiently for the results of the autopsy for Bobbi Kristina Brown. What would the report reveal? Did she die at the hands of Nick Gordon? What role did drugs play in her death? Did she commit suicide? These questions, and many more, were on the minds of many people who were concerned about Bobbi Kristina's tragic demise. Reporters stunned the sea of people who sit by their television, radio, and on social media, to learn the outcome of the medical examiner findings; only, to find out that the report would be sealed.

Bobbi Kris, Forever

The autopsy report was sealed, on September 25, 2015, by the Fulton County Superior Court, and it prohibited the Fulton County Medical Examiner's office from releasing any information to the public. This action was taken to allow more time for the criminal investigation into Bobbi Kristina's death. It seems that the prosecutor's office was concerned that the investigation would be compromised if the report was released. Their major concern, in the criminal investigation, was would the release of the autopsy report cause the perpetrator to flee? Moreover, the prosecutor's office was concerned that witnesses could be endangered by the release of the report.

Bobbi Kris, Forever

This investigation has been pending since before she died. However, there has been no arrest of Nick Gordon; not even for the reports from friends that he brutally assaulted Bobbie Kris on more than one occasion. He brutally assaulted her days before the drowning incident; he assaulted her on the day of the incident and he probably assaulted her on days the family and public did not know about.

After months of waiting for the results, the autopsy report was released on what would have been Bobbie Kristina's 23rd birthday. On March 4, 2016, Judge Henry Newkirk ordered the release of the autopsy report as a result of a motion filed by various media organizations. Bobby Brown did not know anything about the release of the report. He

Bobbi Kris, Forever

found out the report was released, at the same time

the general public found out about the release.

Bobby first acknowledged it was his daughter's

birthday by saying "First and foremost 23 years ago

today, Bobbi Kristina was born. Krissi will always

live in my heart and soul. I love my baby girl."

Then, he voiced his opinion regarding the release of

the report by stating, "For news affiliates to seek

and obtain my daughter's autopsy report, before

anyone is brought to justice for her death is mind

blowing to me. Please pray for my family."

Lots of prayers were needed because the autopsy

report did not yield the results necessary for any

arrests in the case. Bobbie Kristina Brown's

Bobbi Kris, Forever

autopsy report revealed that she died from lobar pneumonia. It is an inflammation of the lobes of the lungs, with an enlargement of the lobe that is most affected by the disease. Karen E. Sullivan, MD and Medical Examiner, determined that the lobar pneumonia was cause by the hypoxic ischemic encephalopathy; which was due to her face being immersed in water and complications of mixed drug intoxication.

The hypoxic ischemic encephalopathy was due to asphyxia, which means not enough oxygen and blood was getting to the brain; which, led to the brain injury. The medical examiner also elucidated the types of drugs found in Bobbi Kristina's body. The lab reports indicated that morphine,

Bobbi Kris, Forever

benzodiazepines (Clonazepam and Alprazolam), marijuana, and the cocaine metabolite (benzoylecgonine) were found in her body . The cocaine metabolite indicated that cocaine had been ingest in the recent days before the drowning incident.

In another section of the report, Bobbie Kristina was described as a 93 pound, thin built and undernourished adult black woman. Her teeth were described as "in an average state of repair" with the left maxillary central and lateral incisors missing. Thus, two of her teeth were missing from her mouth. Also, her left earlobe had four piercing defects, as if her earrings were ripped from her ears. She had three tattoos on her body to signify her undying love for her mother. Furthermore, a multitude of healed scars covered her head, neck, torso and extremities. How did Bobbi Kris get all of those scars on her body?

The medical examiner denoted scars on the head and neck as: one scar on the left side of the upper lip, three scars on the neck, and one scar on the right side of her neck. Furthermore, scars on the torso consisted of two scars on the right side of the upper chest and six scars on the left side of the upper chest. Scars on the extremities included numerous scars on the left and right shoulders and arms.

Bruises were found on her body, but it wasn't specified if the bruises were due to the CPR that was administered the day of the incident or if the bruises resulted from hospital procedures implemented during her hospital stay. What the report did indicate was Dr. Sullivan couldn't determine if the incident was due to an accident or the intentional act of a perpetrator. The medical examiner based her decision on not knowing how Bobbi Kristina entered into the bathtub.

At this point, the most pertinent questions are, "Will the family, friends and public ever know what happened to Bobbi Kristina Brown? Is this just another unsolved mystery? How are Nick Gordon's

Bobbi Kris, Forever

current legal issues with Laura Leal going to impact

the Bobbi Kristina Brown's case?"

Chapter Seven

Amended Civil Lawsuit and Court Judgment

Bobbi Kristina Brown, died on July 26, 2015. On August 7, 2015, Ms. Hargrove amended the original court papers to reflect her untimely demise. According to the amended court document, Nick Gordon's misbehavior caused bodily harm to Bobbi Kristina Brown. He was believed to have administered a toxic cocktail of drugs to Bobbi Kristina and then placed her in a bathtub filled with cold water; which, caused her to have a brain injury. According to the amended court file, he changed clothes and flirted with a female houseguest, after laying his head on her ankle. The houseguest was one of Bobbi Kris' girlfriends, Danyela Bradley.

He commented to the friend, "Now I want a pretty little white girl like you."

According to the amended court document, another friend, Max Lomax, went to check on Bobbi Kristina approximately 15 minutes later and found her under the water in the bathtub; facedown. Curiously, a dust pan was also found in the bathtub, the document denoted. Bobbi Kristina was found in a comatose state, unresponsive, with an engorged mouth and an additional tooth dangling from her mouth.

The document elucidated, that Nick Gordon entered into the bathroom, telling everyone to "clean up." After the others could not revive Bobbi Kris, Nick Gordon begun to slap her; while, performing CPR between slaps. Typically, CPR is performed by blowing two breaths in the person's mouth and then, pumping thirty times on the chest and blowing two more breaths in the mouth. The cycle is repeated until additional help arrives. No where is it written that an unconscious person is slapped between the pumps to the chest area. So, what type of CPR was Nick trained to perform? Furthermore, Michelle Gordon proclaimed that when the paramedics arrived to help Bobbi Kris, no one relieved her son. She maintains that he had to keep administering CPR alone. Any trained person in CPR knows that this is not procedure. Any

Bobbi Kris, Forever

trained person knows that when someone is administering CPR, that person is tired by the time the first responders arrive. The first responders are trained to immediately take over the situation and relieve the person who had been administering the CPR. Now, the questions become, "Was Michelle Gordon telling the truth or was she a victim of her son's lies?"

When she was transported to the hospital, Bobbi Kristina was revived and then placed in medically induced coma to avoid seizures. She was diagnosed with anoxic brain injury, due to a lack of oxygen to the brain. Furthermore, she was said to have global and irreversible brain damage; of which, she later died as the result of the injuries received during the

January 31, 2018 attack on her.

It was determined that while Bobbi Kristina

Brown was in a coma, Nick Gordon transferred

$11, 000 from her bank account into his bank

account. "Really? Is this the type of behavior

someone engages into, when a loved one is sick?"

The amended document specified, as a result of

the toxic cocktail of drugs and the violent attack on

Bobbi Kristina, Nick Gordon caused her demise. He

used his power and influence on her to control

every aspect of who she was as a young woman.

His control over her life was so pronounced that he

even answered her cell phone, watch her every

Bobbi Kris, Forever

move on cameras (installed in her home) and tried

desperately to control her finances. Moreover, he

worked diligently and industriously to keep her

away from family, so that he could control the

money that she inherited from her mother, Whitney

Houston.

Because the case is a civil lawsuit and not a

criminal case, focus was placed on the monetary

damages that Mr. Gordon's behavior caused Bobbi

Kristina and her family. Such expenses included

the cost of her life (which no amount of money can

replace a life), medical expenses and funeral

expenses. The amended file maintains that the court

should consider that if Bobbi Kristina had lived a

long, full and productive work life, she would have

Bobbi Kris, Forever

made astronomical economic gains. Furthermore, it

was documented that the loss of her life prematurely

has led to economic loss.

Nick Gordon was summoned to court to address

the civil/wrongful death lawsuit that was filed

against him. He was a no show for the first court

appearance. So, the hearing was postponed. Again,

he was summons to answer the civil/wrongful death

lawsuit that was issued by the Fulton County Courts

in Georgia. Boldly, he didn't appear for the second

time. However, the case continued without him on

November 17, 2016.

Bobby Brown, Bobbi Kristina's father, testified

in the civil/wrongful death case against Nick

Gordon. Her father sought closure through the civil case because criminal charges were never filed against Nick. He wanted Nick Gordon to be found responsible for the death of his daughter. The hearing centered on Bobbie Kristina's talent and what her life could have been had she not died at such an early age.

Bobby Brown disclosed that his daughter had the vocal abilities of her mother and his dancing skills. He further elucidated that his daughter was talented in "acting" as well. In other words, according to her dad, had she lived, Bobbi Kristina, would have been considered a "triple threat" in the entertainment industry.

Bobbi Kris, Forever

Bobby Brown, went on to highlight the role Bobbi Kristina played in the reality shows, "Being Bobby Brown" and the "Houston's: On Our Own". He maintained that she loved being known as a reality star when she was younger; especially around her classmates. Moreover, he referenced the role Bobbi Kris played, "as secretary", in the sitcom "Tyler Perry's For Better or Worse". According to Mr. Brown, Bobbi Kris had been acting long before she made her debut on television. He described "family plays" that she and her siblings would orchestrate for him and Whitney, during their anniversary celebrations and other family events.

Bobby Brown has an unwavering love for his children. The siblings, although they had different

Bobbi Kris, Forever

mothers and the same father, they were a close-knit family. So, when he received a telephone call from the Houston family, regarding Bobbi Kris' welfare, he traveled to Georgia to see his daughter. Once in Georgia, he telephoned Bobbi Kristina. He told his daughter that he would be picking her up, from the townhouse in which she lived. Over the phone, he could hear Nick Gordon saying, "he stays strapped"; which, means he carries a gun. Bobby Brown made the decision not to see his daughter, at that particular time, because he did not want any trouble that would jeopardize his freedom. So, he left Georgia, to return to California, without the full understanding of what was going on with his child and the danger she faced. However, he maintained

Bobbi Kris, Forever

telephone contact with her and felt as though her life situations were getting better until just before she was found comatose and unresponsive. He recalled speaking to Bobbi Kristina and the promise she made to come to California to visit him and her siblings. During the conversation, with her father, she made it clear that she was trying to get away from Nick Gordon. Thus, her plans were to travel to California, to meet with her infamous father, to go into the recording studio, and to lay the groundwork for her recording career. She was a young lady with a plan for her future. She was a young lady who had tired of her man and no longer wanted him around.

Retrospectively, Bobbi Kris had disclosed to a friend that Nick was not the man she thought he was

Bobbi Kris, Forever

and she made an appointment to discuss the
situation with the friend on January 31, 2015;
however, because she was found unconscious and
then, transported to the hospital, the conversation
never occurred. She was scheduled to be with her
family on or around February 2, 2015; just two days
after the drowning incident. Bobbi Kristina never
made it to California. Conversely, she languished in
the hospital and in hospice until her untimely death.

After the Judge T. Jackson Bedford listened to
the details of the case and considered the fact that
Nick Gordon had not shown up in court as
summoned, he ordered that he pay 36 million
dollars to the family and estate of Bobbi Kristina
Brown.

Bobbi Kris, Forever

Chapter Eight

Gone, But Not Forgotten

Although Bobbi Kristina left this earth in a tragic and terrifying manner, her father is committed to using her platform to promote change in the incidence and prevalence of intimate partner violence (domestic violence). He plans, through a nonprofit organization, to work with young girls and women to help them through the crisis of domestic violence. His vehicle for affecting change, in intimate partner violence, was established in his daughter's name.

The Bobbi Kristina's Serenity House, a nonprofit organization, was established by Bobby Brown in

Bobbi Kris, Forever

2015. Its mission is to "provide 24-hour crisis intervention, emergency transitional shelter, access to resources/referral services and advocacy for social change, with expert support services for victims and survivors of domestic violence." Moreover, the organization plans to educate young women about domestic violence. The purpose of the services offered will move its participants from "crisis to confidence". Through life enrichment and empowerment, the Bobbi Kristina's Serenity House, aim is to rebuild the lives of the young girls and women who enter into its program realm.

In honor of Bobbi Kris' memory, a website has been developed to garner financial support for three Serenity Houses to be located in Los Angeles,

Bobbi Kris, Forever

Atlanta and Boston. The public are being asked to donate funds to build the first Serenity House and to generate the needed funding to support programmatic services. Participants, who donate money, to the organization, will become Serenity Supporters.

An online store, has been created to generate proceeds for the Serenity House. Sweat shirts, T-shirts, and buttons are sold through the website. Messages of encouragement and domestic violence prevention emblazon the buttons. The sweat-shirts and T-shirts promote the Serenity House.

The Serenity House Gala was held at the Taglyan Cultural Complex in Hollywood,

California on March 4, 2018. Entertainment notables, in attendance, was Dawnn Lewis, Ray Parker, Jr., Faith Evans, Cedric the Entertainer, Shondrella Avery, Larkin Arnold and many more supporters.

Bobby Brown has made a daily commitment to promoting the Serenity House and ending intimate partner violence. In an Urban View interview, he encourages domestic violence victims and survivors, women, men and young people, to speak out and seek help through the Bobbi Kristina's Serenity House.

Some important words of wisdom are being offered by Bobby Brown. He states, "Women have to start talking and speaking up and telling people

that they're being abused." He further elucidated, "I

think its essential to let somebody else know. Don't

just let them see you with a black eye and telling

them you fell. No, you didn't fall."

Everyone, who has taken the time and made the

investment in purchasing this book, are encouraged

to talk to the members of their families and others in

their inner circle about intimate partner violence.

Help is available. No one has to live in a situation

that is uncomfortable on any dimension: physically,

psychologically, socially or economically. As we

have witnessed domestic violence crosses all social

stratums. It can affect the lives of people from all

walks of life. This writer invokes the social

Bobbi Kris, Forever

consciousness of everyone to aid in the fight against

the mistreatment and abuse of those who feel

helpless in unhealthy domestic situations. Do not

turn a blind eye or lend a deaf ear; instead, help in

whatever way you can by donating money and time

to build the Bobbi Kristina's Serenity House. It is

more than a purpose, it's a responsibility that

belongs to all people with the social consciousness

to save the lives of the suffering. If you contribute

your money, time and efforts to this cause, Bobbi

Kristina will not have lived in vain…. her life will

have an everlasting impact on all of the participants

who receive services through the organization.

"What was meant to destroy, has blossomed and shall forever grow in God's name. Bobbi Kristina

Bobbi Kris, Forever

was the chosen one to bring focus to the

proliferating situations of intimate partner violence

that permeates the various social strata in the

United States. Now we understand God's purpose.

Bobbi Kristina wins in the end. Blessed be the word

and name of the Lord."

Bobbi Kris, Forever

Chapter Nine

Nick Gordon: A Cat with Nine Lives

Since the death of Bobbi Kristina Brown, Nick Gordon has been in the news twice for allegedly abusing Laura Leal, in separate domestic violence incidents.

The first incident of intimate partner violence, against Laura Leal occurred on June 10, 2017. It seems that Nick and Laura were hanging out at the Duffy Sports Bar with friends. In typical Nick fashion, he was drinking and then, became upset with Laura. He accused her of flirting with a friend of his. In his mind, she was trying to "get with" his friend. Sounds familiar? Didn't he also accuse

Bobbi Kristina of cheating on him? It appears, while under the influence of alcohol, Nick experiences delusions of the paranoid type.

After arriving home, Nick and Laura had begun to argue. The arrest report revealed that Nick repeatedly hit Laura in the face and her head with his fist. According to the police report, he fought on Laura throughout the night. The police took pictures that exposed bruises up and down her arms. Laura disclosed that Nick became unwarrantedly jealous because he thought she was trying to hook up with his friend. She constantly told him that she wouldn't do that to him; but, he did not believe her. He told her to leave his premises, but when she tried to do so, he became irate and violent. At that point, he started beating on her. She was trying

desperately to get away from him; but, he refused to

let her leave the apartment So, she tried to use the

computer to send her sister a Facebook message and

he refused to let her use the computer. The report

divulged that she was able to get away from Nick

by escaping into his mother's bedroom.

When she had awaken Michelle Gordon, she

allegedly was able to show his mother the bruises

on her arms. Nick's mother helped Laura to leave

the apartment by taking her to the sister's home.

The sister, then took Laura Leal to the police station

to make a report. After, the report was made,

Laura's sister took her to the emergency room.

Bobbi Kris, Forever

Nick Gordon was charged with battery and false imprisonment. A bail of $150,000 was set by the court. However, the case never reached the point of a trial. Laura Leal dropped all charges against Nick, denying that he assaulted her.

The second and most recent incident of intimate partner violence against Nick Gordon, happened less than a year later, on March 10, 2018. Laura Leal told the police that Nick Gordon had hit her repeatedly, on their way home, from the bar. According to the police report, Nick disclosed, he was the victim of domestic violence. He proclaimed that Laura Leal had hit him and tore his shirt. Moreover, he revealed that Laura had thrown a bottle at him. The police noticed that Laura's lip was swollen and arrested Nick; although he denied

hitting his girlfriend. The bond was set for $500.00

and Nick was told, by the judge, to stay away from

Ms. Leal, upon his release on March 11, 2018.

The court mandated no contact order was

violated eight days later. A family member

contacted the police to report that Laura Leal was

staying in Nick's apartment. The police found her

in the bedroom. Nick explained she had entered

into the apartment using the code, and they were

just hanging out. Laura Leal confirmed the story

and disclosed she did not feel she was in any

danger.

On March 19, 2018, Nick Gordon was re-

arrested for violating the order issued by the courts.

In his defense, Laura Leal wrote a letter to the judge

explaining that she was the blame for the incident.

She elucidated that she has Bipolar Disorder and

Nick should not suffer the consequences of her

actions. She maintained the incident was a

misunderstanding and she is seeking help for her

disorder. In the letter, she also proclaimed that she

suffers from anger management issues.

Subsequently, the domestic violence charges were

dropped against Nick Gordon because the

prosecutor's office decided a viable witness was

needed to continue the case. Laura Leal was no

longer considered a viable witness. The no contact

charges, against Nick Gordon, remains an open

case.

Bobbi Kris, Forever

Chapter Ten

About Intimate Partner Violence

The Center for Disease Control (CDC) describes Intimate Partner Violence (once referred to as domestic violence) as a serious and preventable public health problem that affect millions of Americans. This organization maintains that Intimate Partner violence includes a variety of acts that are perpetrated by a current or former intimate partner. Such acts or behaviors consist of physical violence, sexual violence, stalking and psychological aggression. These behaviors can occur in both heterosexual or homosexual relationships.

The four predominate types of Intimate Partner Violence are as follows: physical violence, sexual violence, stalking and psychological aggression.

The CDC denotes that physical violence includes the use of force that can lead to death, disability, injury or harm. Behaviors included in this grouping are scratching, pushing, shoving, throwing, grabbing, biting, choking, shaking, hair pulling, slapping, hitting, burning, the use of a weapon and the use of restraints.

The second type of Intimate Partner Violence is sexual violence. It is described as any sexual act that is attempted or completed by a partner and without the victim's consent. Rape, penetration of someone or having another person penetrate someone, unwanted penetration, unwanted sexual contact, unwanted exposure to sexual situations like pornography, sexual harassment, and threats of sexual violence is considered to be sexual violence.

Stalking is the third category of Intimate Partner Violence. It is repeated, unwanted, attention and contact that causes fear or concern for the person's safety. This includes sending letters and emails, leaving flowers and cards, watching or following the victim, going into the victim's house or car, and destroying the victim's property.

Psychological aggression is the fourth category of Intimate Partner Violence. Included in this classification is the use of verbal and non-verbal communication with the intent to harm another person mentally or emotionally. Such behaviors as emotional control, name-calling, humiliation, threats, exploitation and mind games are within this group.

In summary, no person has the right to victimize another person. Consent is needed when engaging in particular types of behaviors (like sadism) that could cause harm to another person. When someone files a police report and then recants it, knowing that he or she has been the victim of Intimate Partner Violence, it is almost as if he or she is granting the perpetrator permission to inflict abuse.

Bobbi Kris, Forever

Love doesn't automatically give permission for one person to control another person's entire life. Consent is needed to take control of the person's livelihood. A power of attorney is the document verifying that a person was granted permission for certain actions to take place. Each and every person has the freedom of choice.

If all of the accounts are true about what happened to Bobbi Kristina Brown, she was in fact, abused by Nick Gordon. It doesn't matter that she abused drugs. The research indicates that Intimate Partner Violence is highly prevalent among substance abusers and their partners. Being rich and famous doesn't preclude circumstances from happening in life. Because Bobbi Kristina Brown

Bobbi Kris, Forever

was the child of people with substance use disorders (both mother and father), she was highly likely to become a person with a substance use disorder, too. Just like, skin color transfers genetically from parent to offspring, so does a substance use disorder.

There are a number of other variables that could have activated the gene for her substance use disorder. For example, the environment in which she was nurtured or a number of stressors like seeing family issues being played out in the tabloids and in movies. Moreover, the stress of dealing with her mother's death, having an overbearing boyfriend, money issues (having too much of it at an early age) and being forced to grow up fast

Bobbi Kris, Forever

(within the period in which her mother died) are all

issues to consider.

In our society, we are quick to place blame on

other people because they are not perfect. Yet, we

are not perfect either. Most of us, travel through

life doing the best we can do. Along the way we

make a variety of mistakes and given enough time

we learn not to repeat the same mistakes over and

over again.

Unfortunately, Nick Gordon has not learned

from his mistakes. The bruises found on Laura

Leal, by the police, did not just jump onto her

body. The reality is these bruises were the result of

violence. Denying that a problem exist, only makes

Bobbi Kris, Forever

it worse. Saying, "I'll never do it again" is with good intention, but good intention with out good work keeps the problem buried until it emerges again. On more than one occasion, God has granted the opportunity for Nick Gordon to get help for his problems. He has been in rehabilitation and in jail. This is God's way of telling him that he needs help. There is no shame in admitting that we are not perfect and in need of help from others. Shame comes when we live in denial and do nothing to help ourselves.

Bobbi Kristina Brown is resting in peace now. There is nothing that can be humanly done to bring her back to earth. Her legacy has been revealed to us posthumously. It is my belief that she was sent,

Bobbi Kris, Forever

by God, to make the public aware of substance use disorders and intimate partner violence among young people.

My concluding words are written in the form of a letter to Laura Leal:

April 8, 2018

Dear Ms. Leal:

God created humans to reign supreme over his domain. We have been given the freedom to love and to follow his teachings. In following his teachings, we have been given the intelligence to navigate our environment and to make choices that bring out the best in us.

Bobbi Kris, Forever

A mate is given to bring us joy and happiness. This help mate is our life's companion and if sent by God will bring out the beauty in us. A man's role is to love, to protect and to provide for the woman he's selected to be his companion. His role is to honor his woman, not to beat her. Love doesn't inflict pain. Control inflicts pain. Hatred inflicts pain. You are more important than any man who would bring harm to you. God created you in his beautiful and magnificent image. Learn your self-worth and you will no longer protect Nick through his misbehavior. You can't save Nick…he has to save himself. I am praying for you.

The Author

Bobbi Kris, Forever

www.ingramcontent.com/pod-product-compliance
Lightning Source LLC
Chambersburg PA
CBHW070136260726
48658CB00001B/452